The German Federal Railways celebrates 150 years of railroading in Germany with a parade of trains in Nuremberg, summer of 1985.

D1397642

Published by Prentice-Hall Books for Young Readers
A Division of Simon & Schuster, Inc., Simon & Schuster Building,
Rockefeller Center, 1230 Avenue of the Americas, New York, NY 10020.

10   9   8   7   6   5   4   3   2   1

Prentice-Hall Books for Young Readers is a trademark of Simon & Schuster, Inc.
Manufactured in the United States of America

Library of Congress Cataloging-in-Publication Data
Scarry, Huck.
Aboard a steam locomotive.
Summary: Detailed pictures with captions present the activities, inner
workings, history, and engine types of steam locomotives.
1. Locomotives—Juvenile literature.   [1. Locomotives—Pictorial works.
2. Railroads—Trains—Pictorial works]   I. Title
TJ 605.5.S28   1986   625.2'61   86-16957
ISBN 0-13-000373-5

ABOARD A
STEAM LOCOMOTIVE
a sketchbook

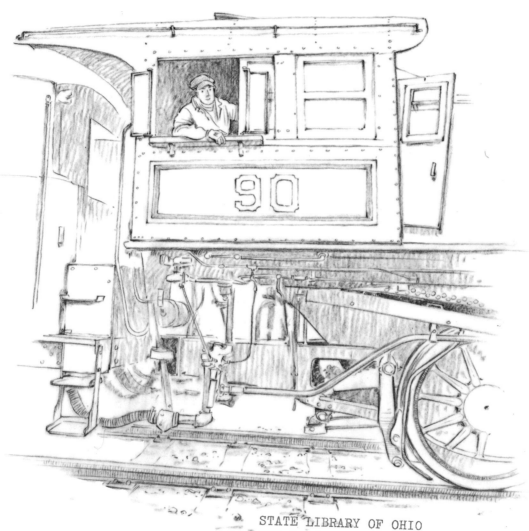

Huck Scarry

Prentice-Hall Books for Young Readers
A Division of Simon & Schuster, Inc., New York

Introduction

As a child, I fell in love with trains. When I began to draw, my pencil often outlined the shapes of a smokestack, cab, wheels, and cowcatcher. And when anyone asked me what I wanted to be when I grew up, I'd reply without hesitation, "A locomotive engineer!"

On rainy days, my friends and I poured over books about steam locomotives, and we played for hours with an electric train set. Although the transformer moved only a small HO-gauge engine around the track, in our minds we were at the throttle driving a powerful one-hundred-ton locomotive!

Of course, none of us had ever really ridden on a steam locomotive, and we had no idea how one worked, or how it was driven.

Since those days of childhood, I have often dreamed of riding on a steam engine to find out what makes it work and what it's like to be aboard. Although steam engines have long disappeared from modern railroads, I knew that steam railroads are run in many different countries for tourists and hobbyists.

So I put on some old clothes, took pencil and drawing paper, and set off on my long-dreamed-of journey, riding steam locomotives in several countries.

87-27863

"Number 90," now on the Strasburg Rail Road

The first thing I learned is that you can locate a locomotive long before you actually see it. You see a plume of brown smoke or a billowy white cloud creeping along the horizon and you know that you have spotted a steam engine.

Depending on which country you are in, the locomotive may look quite different.

"Number 5," now on the Blonay-Chamby Railroad.

Strasburg, Pennsylvania

In Europe, it may be very small and painted in bright colors, while in America it will probably be very big and black. But all the engines are kept spotless and shiny. Some engines are given names, and all of them have numbers. This little French locomotive is known simply as "Number 5."

Number 5 is hissing softly and generating heat like a hot water bottle. The engineer waves to me from the cab and invites me aboard. So I take two giant steps up the ladder, while holding on to the oily brass handrails.

The Blonay-Chamby Railroad, situated on slopes high above Lake Geneva, Switzerland, is narrow-gauge (one-meter gauge, to be precise), and includes a collection of small locomotives and carriages from all over Europe.

"Number 5" is a French locomotive, having been built in Alsace in 1890. Pulling light passenger and freight trains, it was retired in 1934 and started a new life at the construction site of an Alpine dam. Recently found in a children's playground in Austria, it was rescued by Blonay-Chamby railfans. "Number 5," is now the pride of the line!

"Number 5" is an 0-6-0 tank engine, with Stephenson distribution. Built in 1890 by the Société Alsacienne de Construction Mecanique (SACM) Weight: 20 tons. Maximum speed: 25 km/h (15 mph)

I immediately discover that there is not much room for me in the cab, a place obviously designed strictly for work. The engineer tells me to stand in a corner just behind him, well out of the way of the fireman's swinging shovel. My feet wobble as I step on stray chunks of coal.

Though filled with curiosity, I don't dare ask a question. We haven't moved an inch, yet both men are busy as bees. My questions would only add to the confusion of handles, levers, and gauges to which they are giving all their attention.

The whistle gives one short blast, the engineer looks ahead and behind and then gives the throttle a push. I hear a loud "Chuff," then another, and I see that we're on our way.

But I need no eyes to know we are moving, for I *feel* it. Although the engine has springs, it is obvious that we're riding the back of a workhorse pulling the train with all its might. It's like riding on the back of a galloping camel, and it is all I can do to hang on and avoid being poked by pointy tools or burned on sizzling pipes!

The wheels clang on the rails, the smokestack makes deep chuffing noises, the whistle sings, and smoke fills the air. We're moving no faster than a trotting horse...

...but it's as exciting as an express train doing a mile a minute.

4-4-4 Four-cylinder compound express passenger locomotive of the Royal Bavarian State Railways, No. S 2/6 3201.

This engine, built by Maffei of Munich in 1907, could pull passenger trains at 154/kmh (97 mph), a record speed at that time. This engine is displayed today at the Transport Museum, Nuremberg, West Germany.

The Locomotive's Day

The first chore of the day is firing up the engine to heat water in the boiler and produce steam. The fire is lit with oily rags, kindling, and firewood, making a thick cloud of yellowish smoke.

Undisturbed by the choking veil of smoke, a "cleaner" sits atop the engine, giving it a good rubbing down with an oily rag, so it will be nice and shiny on duty.

"Stepney" is an 0-6-0 tank engine, built in 1875 for the London, Brighton, and South Coast Railway (LB&SCR). It now works on the Bluebell Railway in England.

"No. 90" is a 2-10-0 Decapod freight locomotive built in 1924. Formerly of Great Western Railroad in Colorado, it now pulls trains on the Strasburg Rail Road near Lancaster, Pennsylvania.

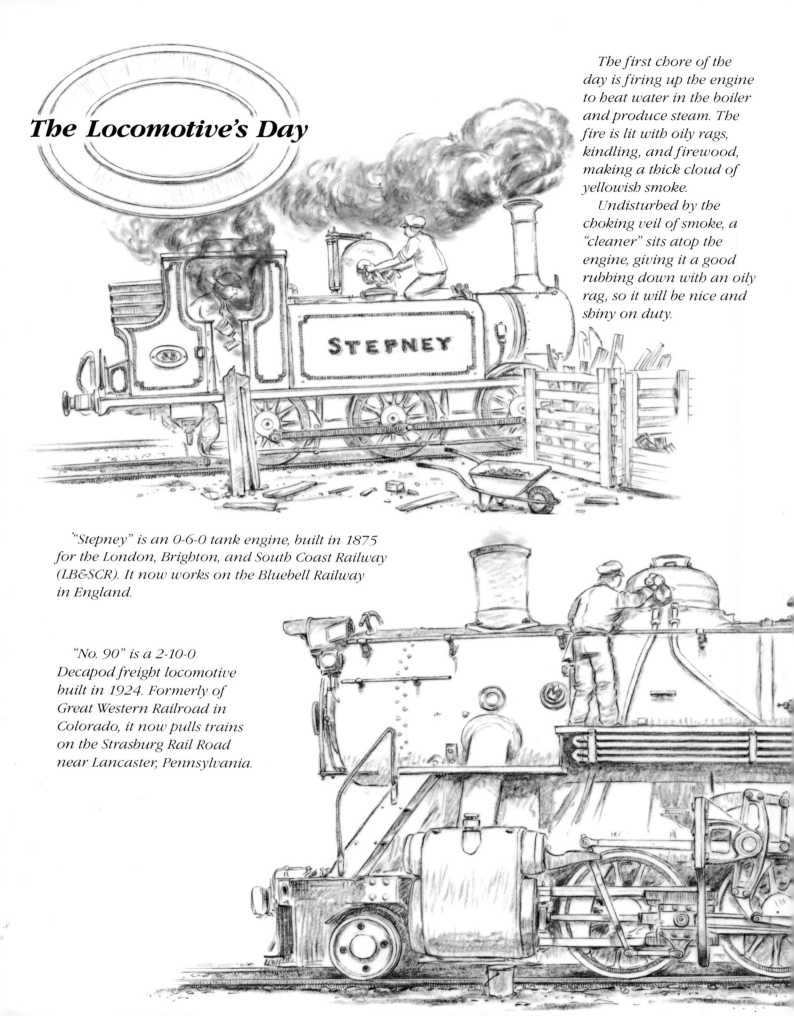

Wherever you find a steam locomotive, the fireman can be heard well before sunrise, breaking up firewood and thrusting it into the firebox onto a crackling fire. The locomotive's workday has begun, although it is still several hours before it will be ready to couple up to its first train.

The locomotive receives more attention than a bride before a wedding. It takes hours to get the fire built up, and the paint and brasswork rubbed down. Dozens of joints need to be greased and oil cups have to be filled to the brim.

You can see that several locomotives are being prepared here. As we go along on our trip, we will sometimes change from one type of engine to another. We will do this so you can see locomotives from other lands. They are all engines I have had a chance to ride and, although they look quite different, the work on board is essentially the same.

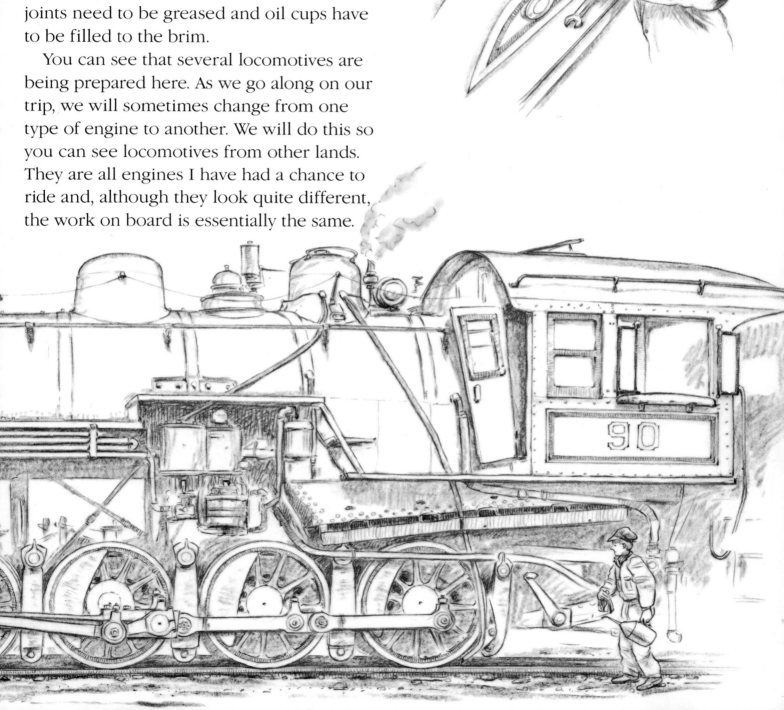

While the fireman is warming up the engine, the engineer has much to attend to. Armed with a wrench, rags, oilcans, and grease sticks, he will begin oiling the engine.

Every single part on the locomotive which moves and is not automatically lubricated will need the engineer's attention before moving off. With dozens of points to check, a good hour or two may pass before the last oil cup has been filled!

Driving grease sticks into connecting rod bearings on "No. 90".

Oiling also gives the engineer a chance to check that nothing's amiss. He is as responsible to his train and passengers as a captain is to his ship.

The water tanks will need topping off, too, so a full supply will be available for the first trip of the day.

"No. 5" gets a drink.

We have plenty of time to wait while the engineer oils moving parts and the fireman tends to the fire and adds to the supply of water. While we wait for the boiling water to give off enough steam to create pressure in the boiler, let's have a look around the engine and familiarize ourselves with its most important parts.

All this while, as water boils in the boiler, steam pressure is building up steadily, as indicated by the steam pressure gauge in the cab. (Maximum pressure in "No. 5" is "12 atmospheres," or twelve times that of the air outside.)

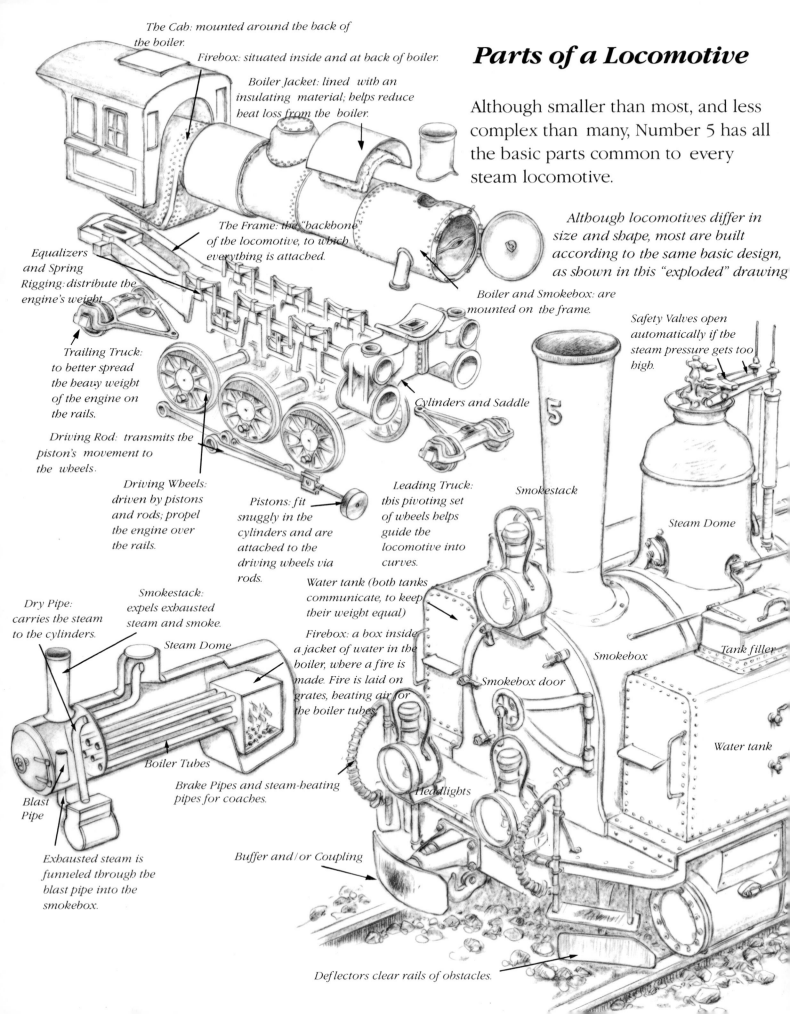

Parts of a Locomotive

The Cab: mounted around the back of the boiler.

Firebox: situated inside and at back of boiler.

Boiler Jacket: lined with an insulating material; helps reduce heat loss from the boiler.

Although smaller than most, and less complex than many, Number 5 has all the basic parts common to every steam locomotive.

Although locomotives differ in size and shape, most are built according to the same basic design, as shown in this "exploded" drawing

The Frame: the "backbone" of the locomotive, to which everything is attached.

Equalizers and Spring Rigging: distribute the engine's weight.

Boiler and Smokebox: are mounted on the frame.

Safety Valves open automatically if the steam pressure gets too high.

Trailing Truck: to better spread the heavy weight of the engine on the rails.

Driving Rod: transmits the piston's movement to the wheels.

Cylinders and Saddle

Driving Wheels: driven by pistons and rods; propel the engine over the rails.

Pistons: fit snuggly in the cylinders and are attached to the driving wheels via rods.

Leading Truck: this pivoting set of wheels helps guide the locomotive into curves.

Smokestack

5

Steam Dome

Dry Pipe: carries the steam to the cylinders.

Smokestack: expels exhausted steam and smoke.

Steam Dome

Water tank (both tanks communicate, to keep their weight equal)

Firebox: a box inside a jacket of water in the boiler, where a fire is made. Fire is laid on grates, heating air for the boiler tubes.

Smokebox

Tank filler

Smokebox door

Boiler Tubes

Brake Pipes and steam-heating pipes for coaches.

Headlights

Water tank

Blast Pipe

Exhausted steam is funneled through the blast pipe into the smokebox.

Buffer and/or Coupling

Deflectors clear rails of obstacles.

If you have been wondering what "0-6-0" or "2-10-0" means, then here is the answer. These numbers refer to the pairs of wheels to be found on the locomotive: leading, driving, and trailing wheels. This wheel classification was devised by Frederic Whyte in 1900.

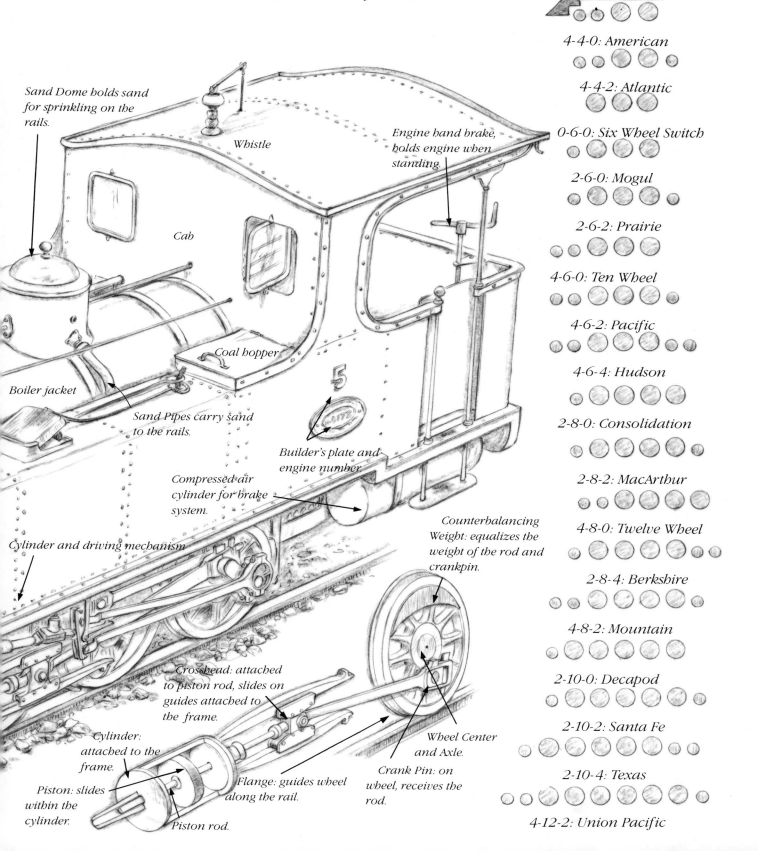

4-4-0: American

4-4-2: Atlantic

0-6-0: Six Wheel Switch

2-6-0: Mogul

2-6-2: Prairie

4-6-0: Ten Wheel

4-6-2: Pacific

4-6-4: Hudson

2-8-0: Consolidation

2-8-2: MacArthur

4-8-0: Twelve Wheel

2-8-4: Berkshire

4-8-2: Mountain

2-10-0: Decapod

2-10-2: Santa Fe

2-10-4: Texas

4-12-2: Union Pacific

Sand Dome holds sand for sprinkling on the rails.

Whistle

Engine hand brake, holds engine when standing.

Cab

Coal hopper

Boiler jacket

Sand Pipes carry sand to the rails.

Builder's plate and engine number.

Compressed air cylinder for brake system.

Counterbalancing Weight: equalizes the weight of the rod and crankpin.

Cylinder and driving mechanism

Crosshead: attached to piston rod, slides on guides attached to the frame.

Wheel Center and Axle.

Cylinder: attached to the frame.

Piston: slides within the cylinder.

Flange: guides wheel along the rail.

Crank Pin: on wheel, receives the rod.

Piston rod.

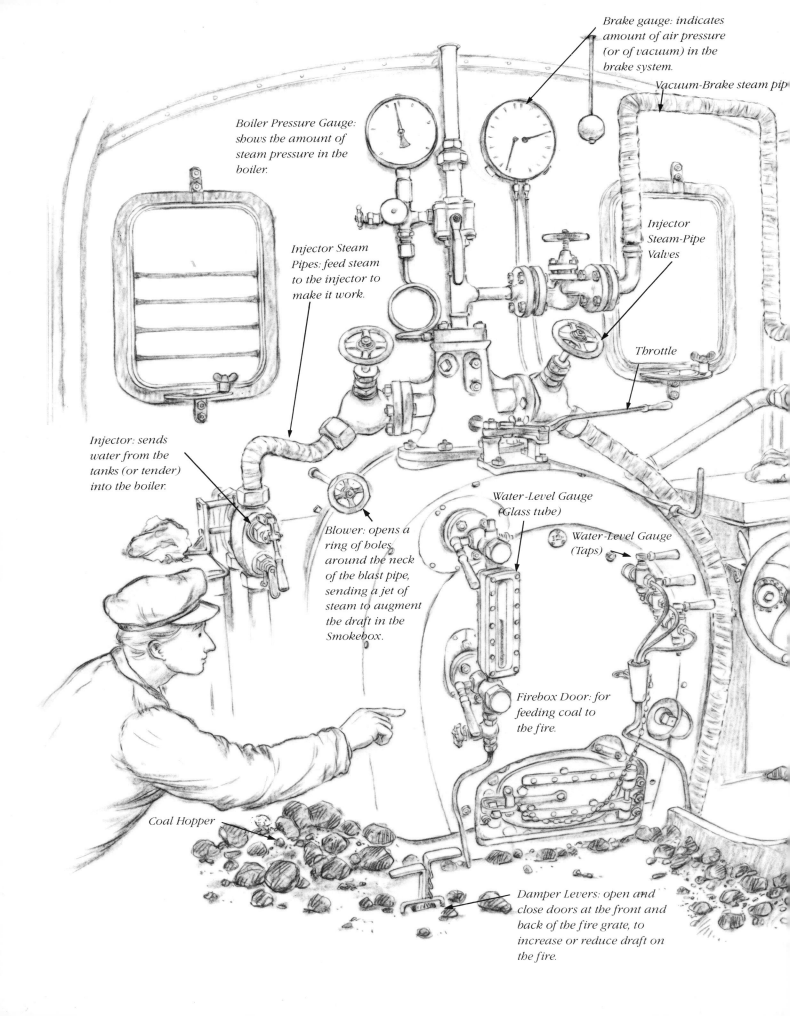

Brake gauge: indicates amount of air pressure (or of vacuum) in the brake system.

Vacuum-Brake steam pip

Boiler Pressure Gauge: shows the amount of steam pressure in the boiler.

Injector Steam Pipes: feed steam to the injector to make it work.

Injector Steam-Pipe Valves

Throttle

Injector: sends water from the tanks (or tender) into the boiler.

Blower: opens a ring of holes around the neck of the blast pipe, sending a jet of steam to augment the draft in the Smokebox.

Water-Level Gauge (Glass tube)

Water-Level Gauge (Taps)

Firebox Door: for feeding coal to the fire.

Coal Hopper

Damper Levers: open and close doors at the front and back of the fire grate, to increase or reduce draft on the fire.

Although at first awesome in their number and variety, the locomotive's controls soon become familiar. The engineer points them out to us here.

Vacuum-Brake Handle

Reversing Wheel (sometimes a lever): for forward and backward motion.

...otplate or Deck

The cab of "No. 5" (dating from 1890)

The cab of a German narrow-gauge tank engine (dating from 1927)

The locomotive's heart is its boiler, its muscle is in its cylinders, and its brain is in the cab. Here all the instruments needed to drive the engine are arranged around the horseshoe shape of the boiler and firebox, within easy reach of the engineer and fireman.

Number 5 is an early engine, so its controls are relatively simple. On a more recent locomotive with more equipment, the engineer might be confronted with nearly as many levers and gauges as the pilot of a modern jet airplane.

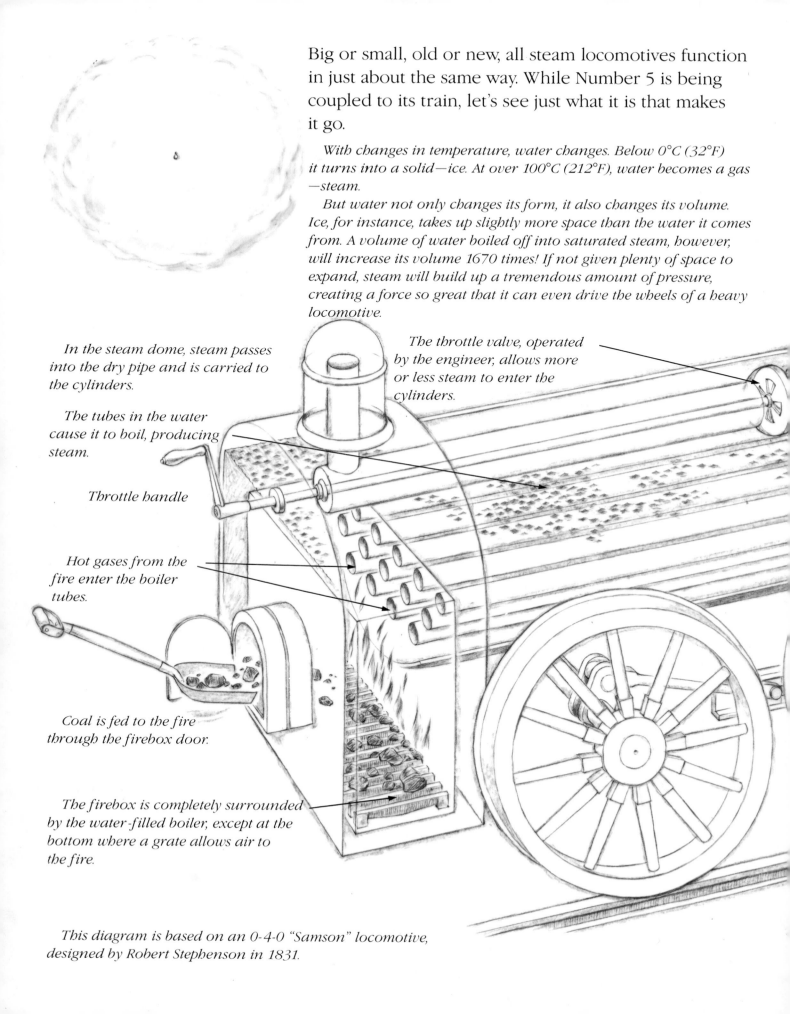

Big or small, old or new, all steam locomotives function in just about the same way. While Number 5 is being coupled to its train, let's see just what it is that makes it go.

With changes in temperature, water changes. Below 0°C (32°F) it turns into a solid—ice. At over 100°C (212°F), water becomes a gas—steam.

But water not only changes its form, it also changes its volume. Ice, for instance, takes up slightly more space than the water it comes from. A volume of water boiled off into saturated steam, however, will increase its volume 1670 times! If not given plenty of space to expand, steam will build up a tremendous amount of pressure, creating a force so great that it can even drive the wheels of a heavy locomotive.

In the steam dome, steam passes into the dry pipe and is carried to the cylinders.

The throttle valve, operated by the engineer, allows more or less steam to enter the cylinders.

The tubes in the water cause it to boil, producing steam.

Throttle handle

Hot gases from the fire enter the boiler tubes.

Coal is fed to the fire through the firebox door.

The firebox is completely surrounded by the water-filled boiler, except at the bottom where a grate allows air to the fire.

This diagram is based on an 0-4-0 "Samson" locomotive, designed by Robert Stephenson in 1831.

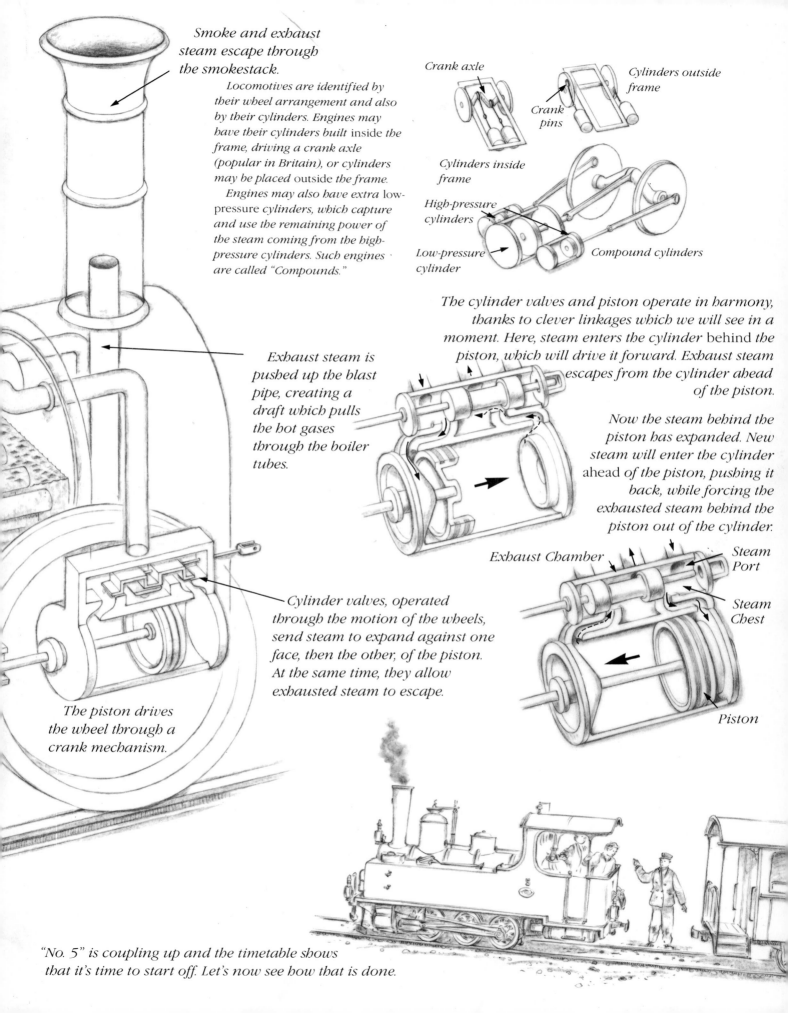

Smoke and exhaust steam escape through the smokestack.

Locomotives are identified by their wheel arrangement and also by their cylinders. Engines may have their cylinders built inside the frame, driving a crank axle (popular in Britain), or cylinders may be placed outside the frame.

Engines may also have extra low-pressure cylinders, which capture and use the remaining power of the steam coming from the high-pressure cylinders. Such engines are called "Compounds."

Crank axle

Cylinders outside frame

Crank pins

Cylinders inside frame

High-pressure cylinders

Low-pressure cylinder

Compound cylinders

The cylinder valves and piston operate in harmony, thanks to clever linkages which we will see in a moment. Here, steam enters the cylinder behind the piston, which will drive it forward. Exhaust steam escapes from the cylinder ahead of the piston.

Exhaust steam is pushed up the blast pipe, creating a draft which pulls the hot gases through the boiler tubes.

Now the steam behind the piston has expanded. New steam will enter the cylinder ahead of the piston, pushing it back, while forcing the exhausted steam behind the piston out of the cylinder.

Exhaust Chamber

Steam Port

Steam Chest

Cylinder valves, operated through the motion of the wheels, send steam to expand against one face, then the other, of the piston. At the same time, they allow exhausted steam to escape.

Piston

The piston drives the wheel through a crank mechanism.

"No. 5" is coupling up and the timetable shows that it's time to start off. Let's now see how that is done.

Moving Off

How does the locomotive back up to hook on to a train, then move forward down the track pulling the train after it? To move the engine forward or backward, the engineer operates the hefty "reversing lever." This lever (and in some cases, a wheel) is linked with a number of rods that set the cylinder valves in precise relation to the piston, sending steam to the desired face of the piston.

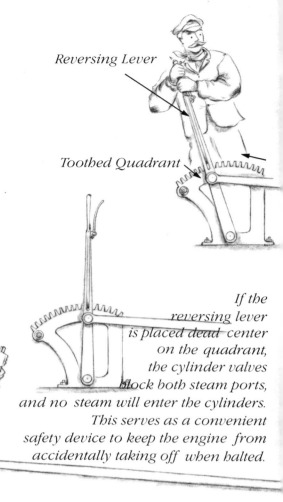

Reversing Lever

Toothed Quadrant

The reversing lever (or revers-ing wheel) operates a system of linkages called the valve gear. The valve gear places cylinder valves in proper relation to the piston, in order to achieve either forward or backward motion of the locomotive.

Furthermore, while the piston (and the wheels) are moving, so do the linkages, so that the valves are constantly adapting their position to maintain the desired motion.

If the reversing lever is placed dead center on the quadrant, the cylinder valves block both steam ports, and no steam will enter the cylinders. This serves as a convenient safety device to keep the engine from accidentally taking off when halted.

To start off, the lever is pushed as far forward as possible. If the rails are wet, the engineer may sprinkle a little sand under the wheels for a better starting grip. After a toot of the whistle, the throttle is opened and steam enters the cylinders from the boiler. Steam pushes the pistons, the pistons turn the wheels...and we're off!

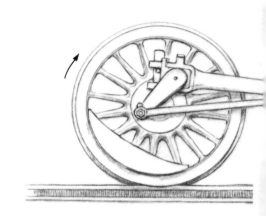

To move forwards, the lever is moved ahead. With the driving rod up, the valves send steam behind the piston, pushing it forward. The rod and the wheel move ahead.

Naturally, when the driving rod is down, the position of the valves changes. This sends steam ahead of the piston, pushing it and the rod back to follow through the forward motion.

To move backwards, the engineer places the reversing lever back. The driving rod is up, so steam is admitted ahead of the piston, pushing it and the rod, and moving the wheel backwards.

When the piston is at full course in the cylinder, the piston rod and driving rod are lined up and there is no driving force. This problem is easily solved by placing the crankpins of wheels on one side of the engine at a different place on the opposite side. While one piston is at the end of its course, the other is right in the middle, pulling the wheels around.

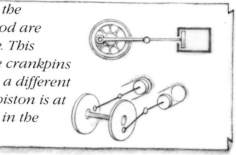

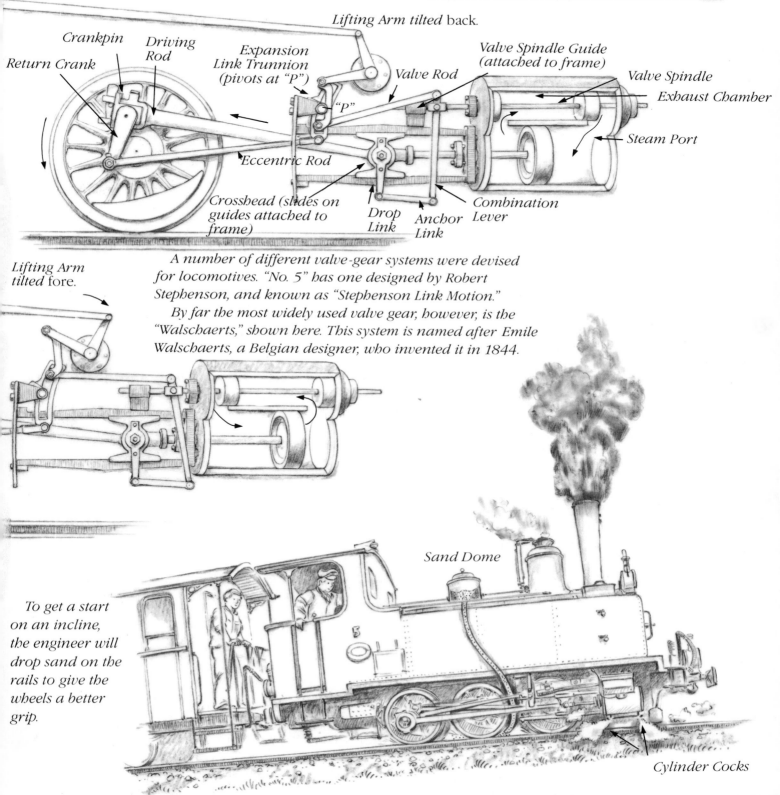

Bridle Rod

Crankpin

Driving Rod

Return Crank

Expansion Link Trunnion (pivots at "P")

Lifting Arm tilted back.

Valve Spindle Guide (attached to frame)

Valve Rod

Valve Spindle

Exhaust Chamber

"P"

Steam Port

Eccentric Rod

Crosshead (slides on guides attached to frame)

Drop Link

Anchor Link

Combination Lever

Lifting Arm tilted fore.

A number of different valve-gear systems were devised for locomotives. "No. 5" has one designed by Robert Stephenson, and known as "Stephenson Link Motion."

By far the most widely used valve gear, however, is the "Walschaerts," shown here. This system is named after Emile Walschaerts, a Belgian designer, who invented it in 1844.

Sand Dome

To get a start on an incline, the engineer will drop sand on the rails to give the wheels a better grip.

Cylinder Cocks

Driving the Locomotive: The Engineer

The engineer can't relax now that we're moving. In fact, his work has just begun. His "iron horse" is every bit as temperamental as a four-footed one. The engine may behave as stubbornly as a mule, or be as skittish as a stallion. Every hill and valley affects the locomotive's performance, so the engineer must constantly check and correct the speed of his machine.

And as if that were not enough, he also has to keep one eye out the window to observe all the signals on the line, and the other eye on his watch to keep on schedule.

Apart from the brake, which we will see later, the engineer works with essentially two controls. These are the reversing lever and the throttle.

Although we have learned that the reversing lever is for moving backwards or forwards, its use, in fact, is far more subtle. Indeed, once underway, the engineer will gradually begin to move the lever back a number of notches on the quadrant. This, of course, alters the relation between the cylinder valves and the piston, actually causing the valves to cut off the supply of steam to the cylinder a bit early. "Cut-off," as this is called, lets a smaller amount of steam expand further within the cylinders. This takes advantage of more of its force, while at the same time reducing the consumption of steam.

"No. 488"

A strong arm is needed for the reversing lever! Later locomotives were fitted with power-assisted levers.

The throttle, on the other hand, is a lever which opens a valve in the steam dome, allowing more or less steam to pass through the dry pipe to the cylinders. Opening the throttle sends more steam—and more power—to the cylinders and causes the engine to accelerate.

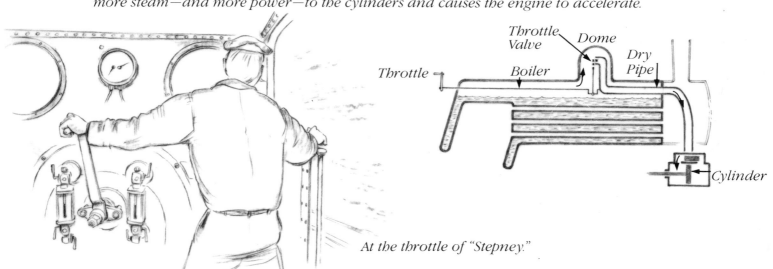

Throttle Valve

Dome

Throttle

Boiler

Dry Pipe

Cylinder

At the throttle of "Stepney."

The engineer has his hands full, with one hand on the throttle and the other on the reversing wheel. The wheel operates just like a lever, engaging a worm screw to move the bridle arm.

"No. 5"

The engineer handles both the reversing lever and the throttle skillfully to get the best performance with the greatest economy. In practice, best economy is gained by running with an open throttle and an early "cut off." This way, a small amount of highly-compressed steam reaches the cylinders and expands fully.

Running the Locomotive: The Fireman

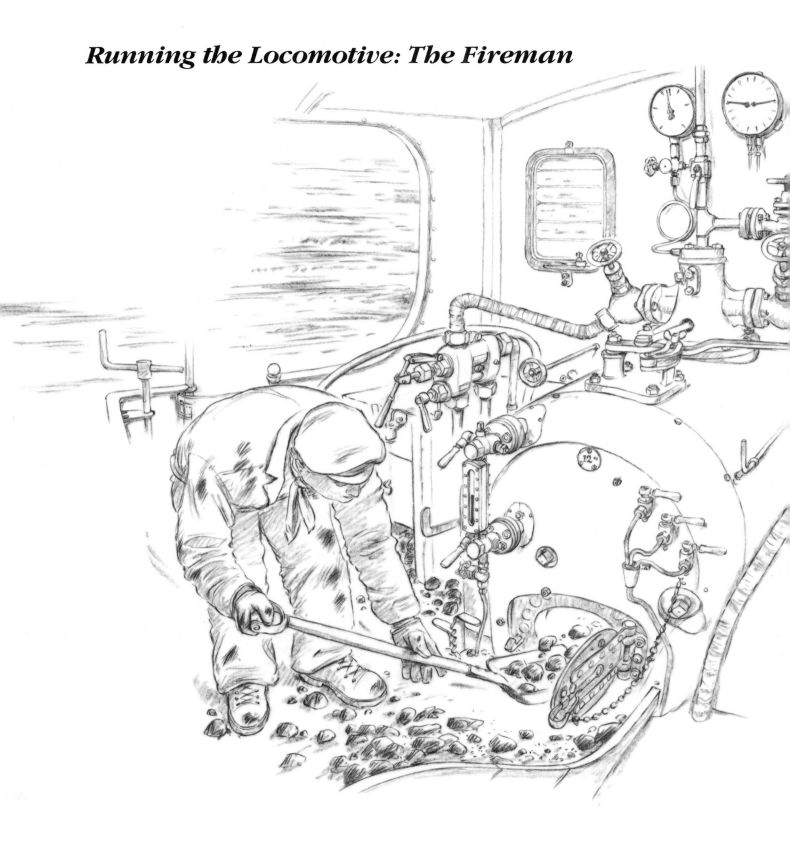

The fireman has to keep a sharp eye on the fire, to be sure that it is burning evenly on the grate. An uneven or slow fire will keep the water from boiling. Too little steam on an incline, for instance, could bring the engine to a halt. So the shovel is always close at hand!

The fireman also keeps an eye on the "glass tubes." These are the water-level gauges mounted on the back of the boiler, indicating the amount of water inside. Since the water is constantly boiling, its level is always sinking. A lack of water would burn the firebox, allowing the steam to expand suddenly, making the locomotive explode.

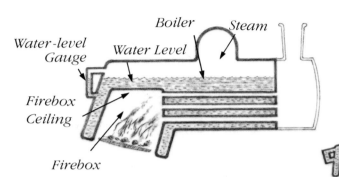

Boiler

Steam

Water-level Gauge

Water Level

Firebox Ceiling

Firebox

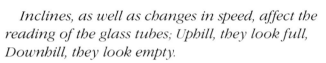

Inclines, as well as changes in speed, affect the reading of the glass tubes; Uphill, they look full, Downhill, they look empty.

The second man on the deck or footplate is the fireman. He does not drive the locomotive, but he keeps it running.

With every stroke of the pistons, steam (from water) is released from the boiler and fuel is burned in the firebox. The fireman's job is to replace what is quickly being used up—more water to the boiler, more coal to the fire.

The fireman's tools are "injectors" (for adding water to the boiler), a shovel, tireless muscles, and an uncomplaining back.

Obviously, water has to be regularly put back into the boiler. This is done with the "injector," invented by the Frenchman, Henri Giffard, in 1858. The injector is a clever device for feeding water into a boiler whose pressure inside is several times as great as that outside.

Because it is perhaps the most vital instrument for the running of the machine, as well as for its safety, most locomotives are fitted with two injectors.

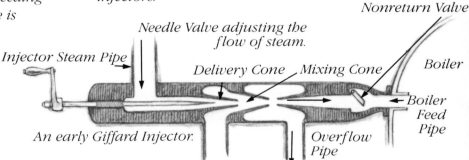

Nonreturn Valve

Needle Valve adjusting the flow of steam.

Injector Steam Pipe

Delivery Cone   Mixing Cone

Boiler

Boiler Feed Pipe

An early Giffard Injector.

Overflow Pipe

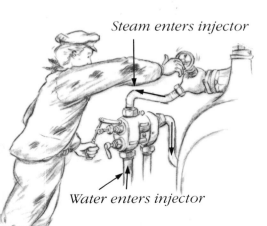

Steam enters injector

Water enters injector

Steam from the boiler is admitted to the injector, where it picks up, and mixes with, water arriving from the tanks (or tender). This mixture is then funnelled through a series of fixed cones which augment, and then suddenly decrease, the water's speed.

The deceleration increases the water's pressure, so that it is actually greater than the pressure in the boiler, which it enters through a one-way "nonreturn" valve.

The fire is burning fiercely, the steam pressure is up, the track is level, and the signal reads "all clear." Both engineer and fireman can rest for just a minute and enjoy the thrill of speed.

"No. 488" barrels through gentle English countryside, on the Bluebell Line.

One accessory found only on British locomotives is the teapot! Both the engineer, and the fireman, hang a white enameled tin conveniently beside the water-level gauges on the back of the boiler where their brew is kept piping hot.

Signals

Now that we're running so nicely, a new problem presents itself. Although we cannot see it, we are sharing our track with other locomotives. They are moving just as fast as we are, and perhaps they are even moving right toward us.

Our locomotive is kept from meeting another (with a crash) by signaling. Here is how it works.

A simple system is the use of a "token." Only one train is allowed on a section of track at a time: the one possessing the token. This is normally a piece of metal which the engineer picks up at the beginning of the section, and drops off at the end of the section, where it can be picked up by another engine, to enter the line. A token is like a unique ticket providing admission to a section of track.

Token System

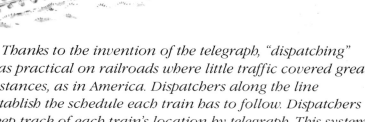

Thanks to the invention of the telegraph, "dispatching" was practical on railroads where little traffic covered great distances, as in America. Dispatchers along the line establish the schedule each train has to follow. Dispatchers keep track of each train's location by telegraph. This system works solely on the observance of time schedules—there are no signals.

Dispatching System

Block System

This system is best for busy railroads carrying heavy traffic. Essentially, the line is divided up into "sections," each section being governed by a set of signals. Only one train at a time is allowed in a section, so that if the signals are observed, accidents should never happen.

Block

Block

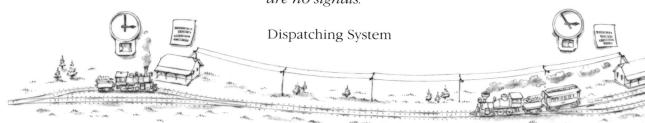

Block

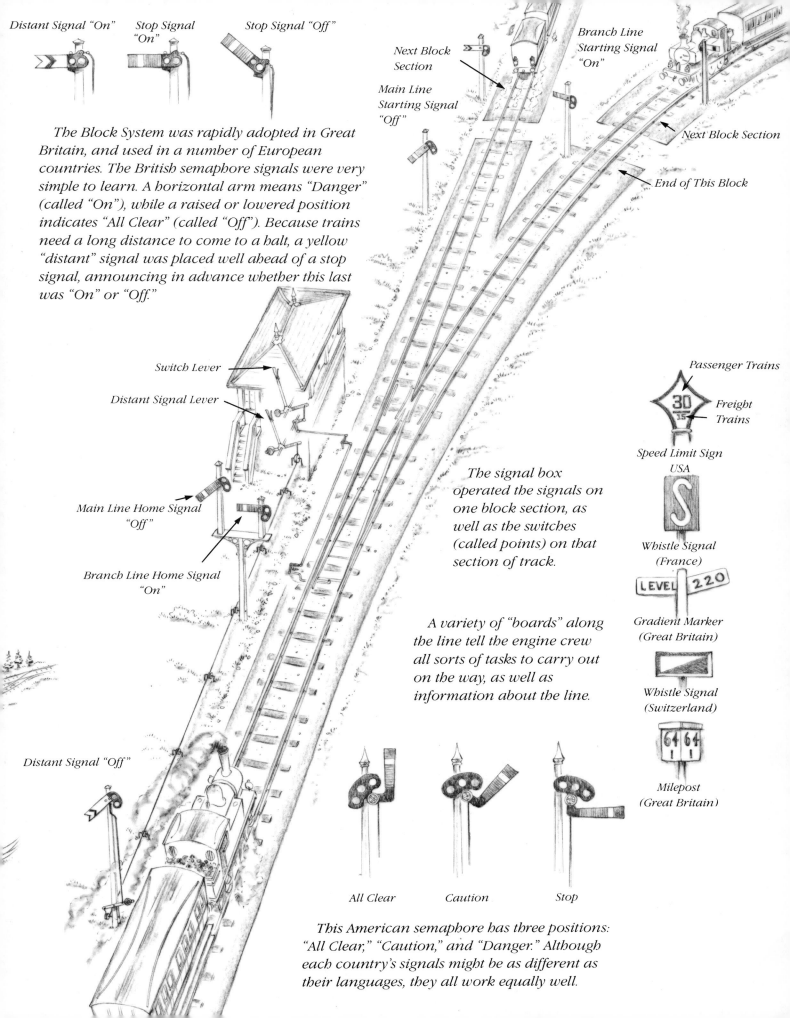

Distant Signal "On"

Stop Signal "On"

Stop Signal "Off"

Next Block Section

Main Line Starting Signal "Off"

Branch Line Starting Signal "On"

Next Block Section

End of This Block

The Block System was rapidly adopted in Great Britain, and used in a number of European countries. The British semaphore signals were very simple to learn. A horizontal arm means "Danger" (called "On"), while a raised or lowered position indicates "All Clear" (called "Off"). Because trains need a long distance to come to a halt, a yellow "distant" signal was placed well ahead of a stop signal, announcing in advance whether this last was "On" or "Off."

Switch Lever

Distant Signal Lever

Main Line Home Signal "Off"

Branch Line Home Signal "On"

The signal box operated the signals on one block section, as well as the switches (called points) on that section of track.

A variety of "boards" along the line tell the engine crew all sorts of tasks to carry out on the way, as well as information about the line.

Passenger Trains

Freight Trains

Speed Limit Sign

Whistle Signal (France)

USA

Gradient Marker (Great Britain)

Whistle Signal (Switzerland)

Milepost (Great Britain)

Distant Signal "Off"

All Clear

Caution

Stop

This American semaphore has three positions: "All Clear," "Caution," and "Danger." Although each country's signals might be as different as their languages, they all work equally well.

The signals are operated by signalmen stationed in signal boxes along the line. A signalman regulates the traffic along a section of track, as a policeman governs traffic at a crossroad. The signalman listens to electric bell signals sent to him by signalmen in other boxes. The bell messages inform him of train traffic up and down the line. The signalman can pull levers, operating signals, or switches (called points) for the safety of the trains. He can signal trains to stop or go, and he can switch a train to a different track.

Today, of course, signaling is done electronically, and one box may handle many lines. But this is how it was done in England in the days of steam.

Plan of the Block Section governed by this "box," with all its sidings.

Shunting indicator. This receiver tells the signalman what movements are taking place on the sidings.

SHEFFIELD PARK

Fortunately, the telegraph was invented in the early days of railroads. Electric code messages could be tapped out by one signalman and received by a bell ringing at the next signal box.

A toggle switch on block instruments could be used to indicate different messages, depending on which way the switch was moved. Moving the switch up or down moved a similar switch on a receiver at the next box, giving the desired message.

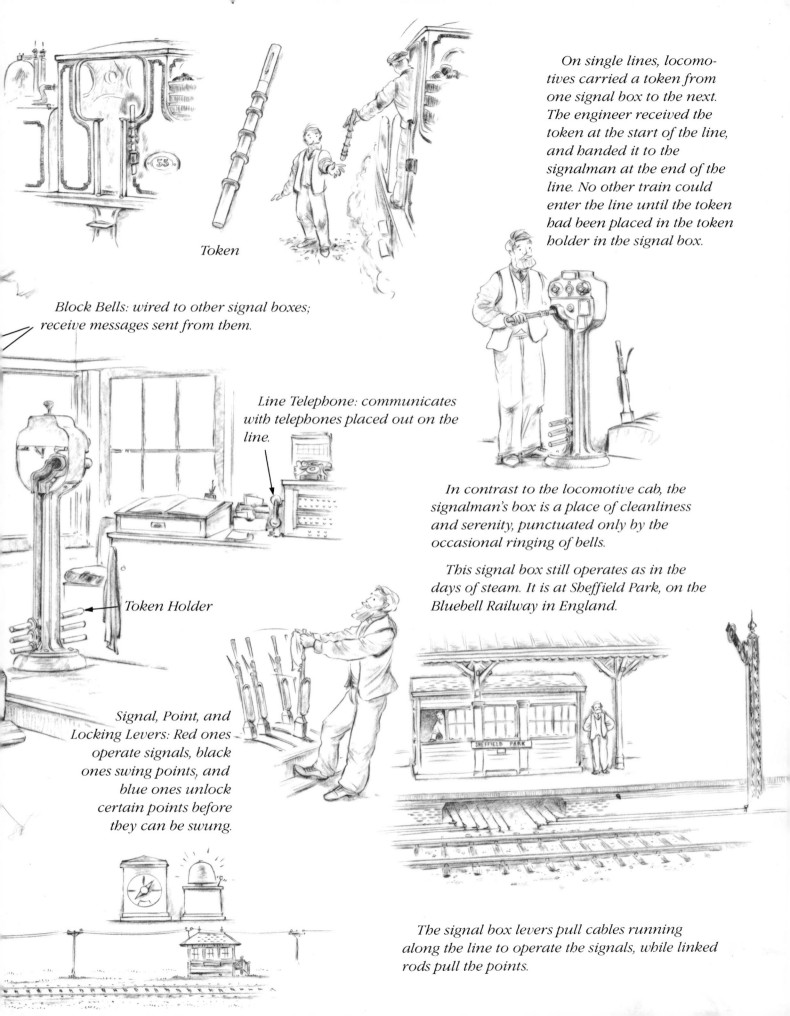

Token

On single lines, locomotives carried a token from one signal box to the next. The engineer received the token at the start of the line, and handed it to the signalman at the end of the line. No other train could enter the line until the token had been placed in the token holder in the signal box.

Block Bells: wired to other signal boxes; receive messages sent from them.

Line Telephone: communicates with telephones placed out on the line.

Token Holder

In contrast to the locomotive cab, the signalman's box is a place of cleanliness and serenity, punctuated only by the occasional ringing of bells.

This signal box still operates as in the days of steam. It is at Sheffield Park, on the Bluebell Railway in England.

Signal, Point, and Locking Levers: Red ones operate signals, black ones swing points, and blue ones unlock certain points before they can be swung.

SHEFFIELD PARK

The signal box levers pull cables running along the line to operate the signals, while linked rods pull the points.

The signals are at "All Clear" for "No. 488."

Hills and Dales

On tracks wet with rain, or sprinkled with leaves, the engineer will make up for the slippery surface by using the sander.

A locomotive is like a bicycle rider trying to pedal up a steep hill. Both need to use all their strength to get over the top without stalling. On the steep downward slope, they also need some way to lower their speed, so they won't race out of control. Here is how the engine crew copes with the ups and downs of the line.

As it rises and falls on inclines, the locomotive's water always remains level, which can give a false reading in the glass tubes.

On most downhill stretches, the engine will simply be allowed to coast, throttle shut, while the engineer uses the brakes to prevent a runaway engine.

But on very long descents, the locomotive's pistons can actually act as brakes themselves. By setting the reversing lever back and opening the throttle, the pistons compress against the steam in the cylinders and check any acceleration.

Throttle Closed

Lever Back

and

Throttle Open

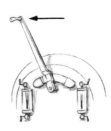

Injector On

Lever Forward

Throttle Open

Tackling a hill is a test of strength and skill for the engine crew. For maximum power, the throttle is set full open, while the reversing lever is placed well forward. Since steam is quickly being used up with each uphill stroke, the fireman is kept on his toes to maintain a good water level in the boiler, as well as a good fire, to keep steam pressure as strong as possible.

Shovel, Shovel, Shovel!

When the tracks are level, both crew and machine can rest. To conserve steam, the reversing lever is pulled back several notches and the throttle is set to maintain just the right speed.

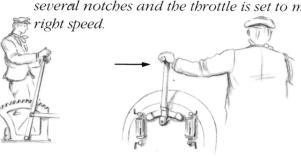

Knowing that a descent is approaching, the fireman tops off the boiler again, to be sure that the firebox ceiling is still covered with water, in spite of the downward slope of the boiler.

Water

On a long journey, a powerful locomotive will drink thousands of gallons of water. Water tanks mounted on the locomotive would be too small, requiring the engine to make frequent stops along its route for refills. That is why big locomotives are provided with a "tender." A tender is a separate railroad car built to store a large amount of water and fuel. It's not too different from a hiker's backpack.

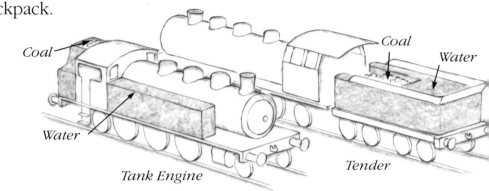

A small tank engine like "No. 5" or "Stepney" may need only a few refills of water during its day's work. So water towers are placed at several station stops along the line.

Bigger locomotives, consuming far more water, are designed with copious tenders to avoid frequent stops for a drink.

European water towers are operated from the ground. The engineer opens the tap below, while the fireman, standing atop the tender, tells him when to turn it off before it overflows and gives him a cold shower!

Elevated towers are typical features of American railroads, and the tender can easily be filled by just one man.

Coal

Water

Tank Engine

Coal

Water

Tender

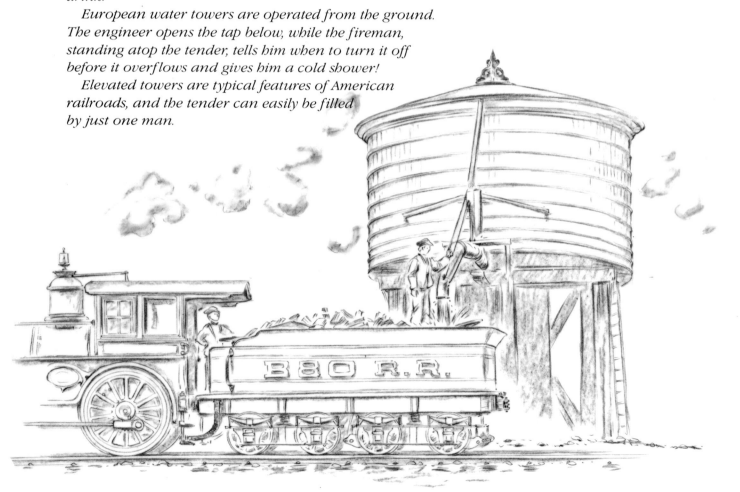

B&O R.R.

On long express runs, where no stops for refills are desired, tenders can scoop up water from troughs laid between the rails. This clever arrangement was invented in England in 1858.

This board tells the engine crew that they are approaching a water trough. 'Time to crank down the scoop!'

Water is held in the open-ended troughs by laying them on a gentle slope along the line. (The troughs are really much longer than shown in these drawings).

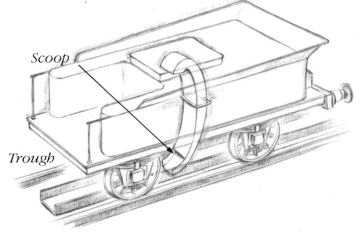

Scoop

Trough

Stop!

The extended arm and red light of the signal ahead commands the engineer to bring his train to a halt. Fortunately, the several hundred tons of speeding metal at his command can be easily stopped, thanks to the Westinghouse air brake. Here is how it works.

The brake handle is placed within easy reach of the engineer.

Clearly visible outside on many locomotives are one or more air compressors. These work automatically to provide a constant supply of compressed air to the braking system.

Compressed air produced aboard the locomotive is stored in a main reservoir usually visible on the locomotive. A compressed-air pipe runs from the engine's reservoir to the brake handle (which is a valve to close the pipe), and on through to the entire train via flexible hose couplings between the coaches. The pipe is closed at both ends of the train.

The compressor is powered by steam from the boiler which presses on a double piston, pushing it down to compress air, which is then sent to a special reservoir on the locomotive for storage.

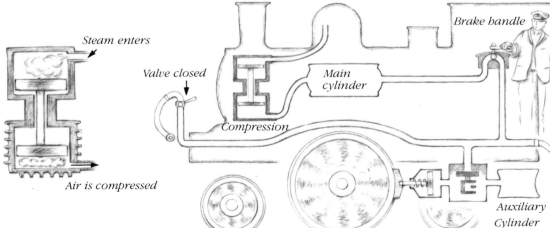

Steam enters

Valve closed

Air is compressed

Steam dome

Brake handle

Main cylinder

Compression

Auxiliary Cylinder

When the air brake is Off, compressed air pressure is maintained in the air pipe running through the train. The special triple valves are held down by this pressure, so the auxiliary reservoirs are also filled with compressed air.

When the brake is pulled on, it blocks the air supply from the main reservoir and compressed air escapes from the pipe. Triple valves now place the auxiliary reservoirs in communication with the brake cylinders, applying pressure to the pistons and on to the brakes.

When the brake is turned off, the valves move back and new air is admitted to the auxiliary reservoirs ready to work again.

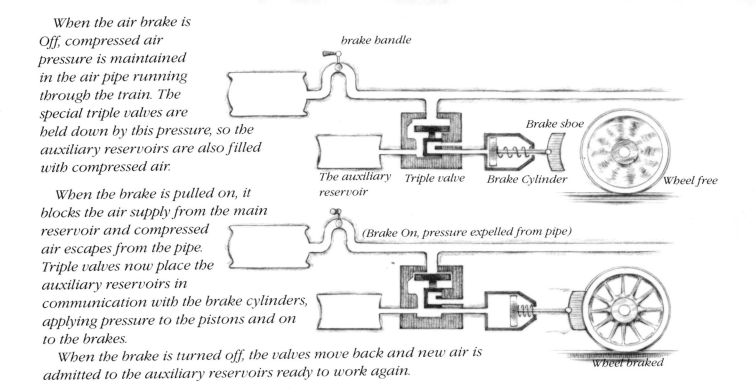

brake handle

Brake shoe

The auxiliary reservoir

Triple valve

Brake Cylinder

Wheel free

(Brake On, pressure expelled from pipe)

Wheel braked

A manual brake handle is often found on locomotives to hold the engine firmly in place, once stopped.

air pipe

Vacuum brakes use a rush of steam to create a vacuum in a special cylinder. Atmospheric pressure outside pushes a piston into the vacuum, applying the brake shoe.

Beneath an American coach from the turn of the century can be seen:

Auxiliary reservoir (on locomotive and on each coach)

Compressed-air pipe (runs through entire train)

The brake cylinder

A brake piston rod

The triple-valve housing

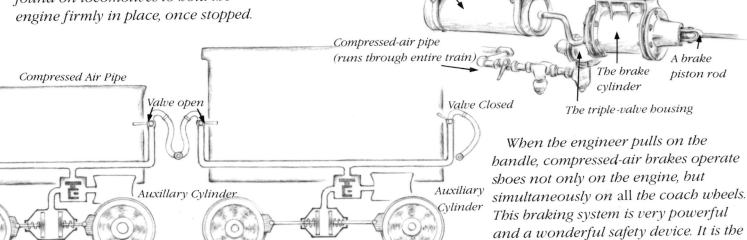

Compressed Air Pipe

Valve open

Auxiliary Cylinder

Valve Closed

Auxiliary Cylinder

When the engineer pulls on the handle, compressed-air brakes operate shoes not only on the engine, but simultaneously on all the coach wheels. This braking system is very powerful and a wonderful safety device. It is the invention of George Westinghouse, who developed it in America during the 1860s.

Cleaning Up

Our locomotive trip is over, and although the last train of the day has been brought safely to its destination, the engine crew's workday is still not done.

Back at the shed, the locomotive will need to be filled with coal and water, and cleaned of ashes, so that it will be ready for work again in the morning.

The engineer will give his machine a final inspection, looking for anything that might be wrong. Only when he is satisfied that his engine is in good shape will he be able to think about a rest for himself and a hot shower.

"Stepney"

Just like a fireplace, an engine's firebox needs to be cleaned of ashes and tenacious, crusty "clinkers" left by coal.

The water tanks (or tender) need to be filled, too, so a supply of water will be ready for "firing up" next morning.

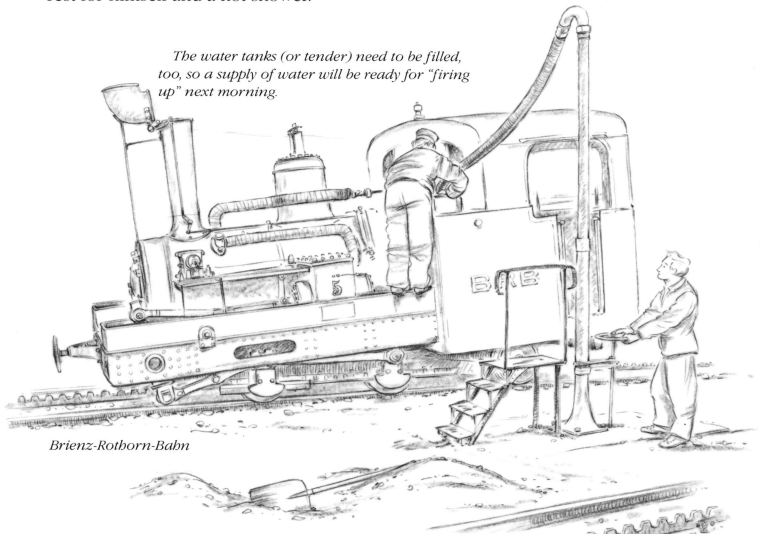

Brienz-Rothorn-Bahn

At the ash pit, the ash pan beneath the grates will have to be thoroughly cleaned…anything but a clean job!

There will also be a stop at the coal bunker, to replenish our fuel.

"No. 5"

Up front, the smokebox door is opened in order to clean the smokebox of ashes.

"Stepney"

At long last, the locomotive is ready to return to its shed for the night, ready for another busy day of duty tomorrow morning!

*The roundhouse
with its turntable
was a common sight
on all railroads,
in the days of steam.*

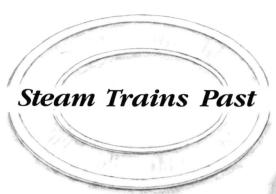

Steam Trains Past

Becoming an Engineer

Hierarchy in the engine shed:

Foremen: responsible for the maintenance of the engine fleet.

Assistants: made sure their foreman's orders got through.

Engineers: were boss on the deck (footplate).

Firemen: added fuel and water and were responsible to their engineers.

Cleaners: boys hoping one day to trade their rags for a fireman's shovel.

An icy January morning: 3 a.m. Young boys give "Stepney" a rubbing down.

Here is how work tasks were organized in locomotive sheds in Great Britain in the days of steam.

In the days of steam, the dream of many children was to become a locomotive engineer. In the days before the invention of the automobile and the airplane, engine crews could boast that they drove the fastest machines on earth.

But because so much skill was needed to drive an engine, it took many years of training before a youngster was allowed on the deck. Like the young sailor who aspires to become a captain, the young railwayman had to learn many things before achieving the dream of holding the throttle.

Shed Laborers: carried out the dozens of sundry jobs and repairs around the locomotives.

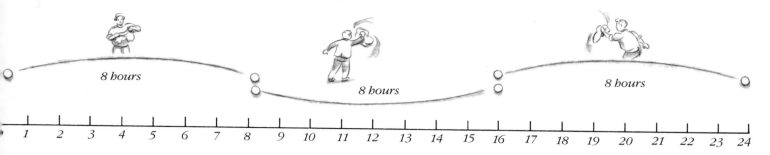

8 hours   8 hours   8 hours

| 1 | 2 | 3 | 4 | 5 | 6 | 7 | 8 | 9 | 10 | 11 | 12 | 13 | 14 | 15 | 16 | 17 | 18 | 19 | 20 | 21 | 22 | 23 | 24 |

Boys started their railroad careers as cleaners, rubbing locomotives to spotless splendor with oily rags. Working various combinations of 8-hour shifts to fill a 72-hour workweek did not leave much time for play, nor did the skimpy pay permit buying much.

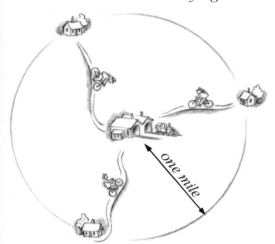

one mile

When a young man graduated from "cleaner" to fireman, he was not allowed to live any farther than a mile from the shed, so he could be quickly fetched for duty on the footplate at any time.

Well before the first trip of the day, he had to fire up the engine on his own time and without pay.

STE

The moment the engine was set in motion, so too, was the fireman. Injecting water and shoveling coal was good for body builders, but it was also back breaking!

As locomotives grew in size, so did their fireboxes. Some locomotives ate so much coal that the fireman had to shovel nonstop from the beginning of a trip to the end. There was no time to put the shovel down and take a rest!

After working years on the footplate as a fireman, a man might be lucky enough to become an engineer...provided he could pass the eyesight test!

The Engineer's Day

Like so many jobs in the nineteenth century, a job on the railroad was hard, with long hours and small pay. The engineer's job, however, was especially rough. Because they were always on call every day at any time, engineers did not have much leisure. Those who operated long-distance locomotives might have to stay away from home several nights a week, sleeping in a railway hostel far away from home.

The engineer was on call every day, any time. A "knocker" mounted on a bike would arrive without notice, and summon the engineer to the shed.

The fireman turned engineer became locked in a world where he appeared little different from the gears and levers of the machine he drove. Once married to the footplate, his life became no more than just keeping on schedule!

Although paid for a twelve-hour shift, the engineer might not be able to leave his footplate for twice that time. If not called one day, he received no pay for it. Nor was he paid for work on Sunday, even though he may have worked all 24 hours of it!

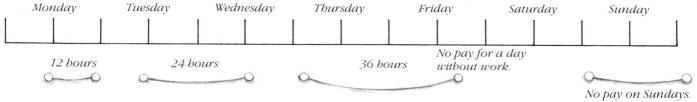

| Monday | Tuesday | Wednesday | Thursday | Friday | Saturday | Sunday |

12 hours   24 hours   36 hours   No pay for a day
                                                                without work.

No pay on Sundays.

While the fireman douses the coal to prevent dust, the engineer oils "No. 488."

At first, engine crews were assigned to one engine, which they might man for years. But with the growth of railroads in Britain, engine crews had to work over longer distances and at the end of duty were miles from home. "Lodging" became common practice, with engine crews overnighting in grim and Spartan railway hostels.

"Overnighting," of course, might mean catching only a few hours of sleep. As to the hostel beds, they were always warm. As soon as one engine man rose from his sleep, another exhausted one would crash down in his place! In America crews slept in the caboose.

A hostel

The Birth of the Steam Locomotive

The first stationary steam engine in operation was built by Thomas Newcomen, an Englishman. It was used for pumping water from mines. Although slow, and an inefficient user of energy, it led the way to the much improved machines of James Watt, a Scotsman, who patented his steam engine design in 1769.

Steam engines were soon put to use not only for operating pumps, but also for driving machinery in factories, for propelling boats, and before long, to drive road, and rail locomotives, too.

Newcomen's steam-powered pump of 1712. Drawn from a model in the Smithsonian Institution.

The first land vehicle run by steam was that built by the Frenchman Nicolas Cugnot. He hoped to sell his machine as an artillery wagon. Although he ran it in 1769 and 1770, he could never travel very far before running short of steam.

Cugnot's artillery wagon, now on display at the National Conservatory of Arts and Crafts in Paris.

The very first steam engines did not roll on tracks at all. They were not locomotives, but stationary engines designed for pumping water out of mine shafts.

Steam engines were first used successfully for propulsion in the early 1800s to move ships called paddle wheelers. But as early as 1769, a Frenchman named Nicolas Cugnot built a steam wagon that moved along under its own power for a few feet. Soon inventors tried to design a workable steam carriage.

Notable among them was the Englishman Richard Trevithick, who built several "road locomotives." In 1804, he built and ran one of his locomotives on a mining railway in Wales, pulling a load of 10 tons and 70 men. His feat inspired others to do better still, and locomotives were soon being built elsewhere in England.

Railways themselves are far older than locomotives. Early illustrations show that mining wagons ran on rails in the mid 1500s. Horses were used to pull the wagons before the invention of the "iron horse."

A pioneer of the locomotive was Richard Trevithick, an Englishman who designed and built several road locomotives. Having accepted a challenge to see if he could make a locomotive to pull a train of coal wagons, he won his bet when his engine pulled a trainload of men along the "Pen-y-Daren Plate-Way" in Wales, in 1804.

A serious problem of early railroad locomotives was that their great weight often broke the brittle cast iron rails. But rapid improvements to both machine and rail soon established the railroad locomotive as a practical, powerful, and reliable workshorse.

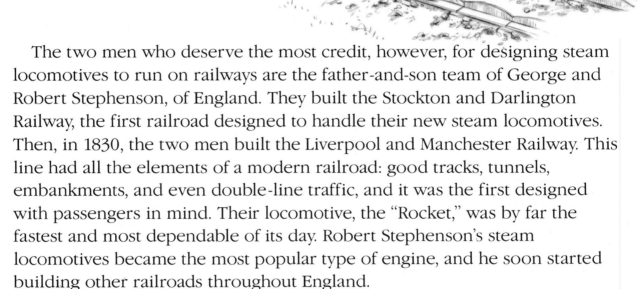

The two men who deserve the most credit, however, for designing steam locomotives to run on railways are the father-and-son team of George and Robert Stephenson, of England. They built the Stockton and Darlington Railway, the first railroad designed to handle their new steam locomotives. Then, in 1830, the two men built the Liverpool and Manchester Railway. This line had all the elements of a modern railroad: good tracks, tunnels, embankments, and even double-line traffic, and it was the first designed with passengers in mind. Their locomotive, the "Rocket," was by far the fastest and most dependable of its day. Robert Stephenson's steam locomotives became the most popular type of engine, and he soon started building other railroads throughout England.

George Stephenson opens the Stockton & Darlington Railway which he built in 1825, driving his engine "Locomotion."
Although this line was designed to pull coal wagons, passengers were also carried, opening the way for the modern passenger railroad.

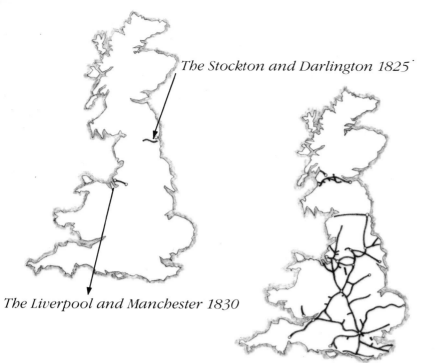

The Stockton and Darlington 1825

The Liverpool and Manchester 1830

Only a dozen years since the opening of the Stockton & Darlington, the first railroads appeared in Europe.

Railroads were also built rapidly in the United States, so fast that by 1840 there were already 2800 miles of track!

Some early British railways included the:
Stockton & Darlington, 1825
Liverpool & Manchester, 1830
Canterbury & Whitstable, 1830
London & Greenwich, 1836
London & Birmingham, 1838

The "John Bull" was built at Robert Stephenson's locomotive works for the Camden & Amboy Railroad in 1831.

However, it was too heavy for the lightweight tracks in America and had to be extensively modified. It was even given the world's first "cowcatcher"! The "John Bull" can be seen today at the Smithsonian Institution, Washington, D.C.

Early European railroads were the:
St. Etienne-Andrézieux and
    St. Etienne-Lyons, France, 1832
Nürnberg-Fürth, Germany, 1835
Brussels-Maline, Belgium, 1835
Paris-St. Germain, France, 1837
Vienna-Wagram, Austria, 1837
St. Petersburg-Pavlovsk, Russia, 1837
Naples-Portici, Italy, 1839

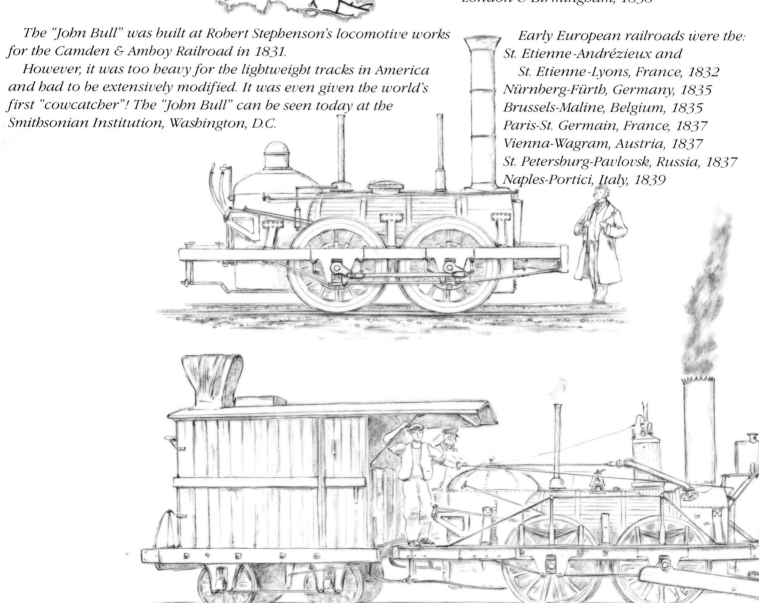

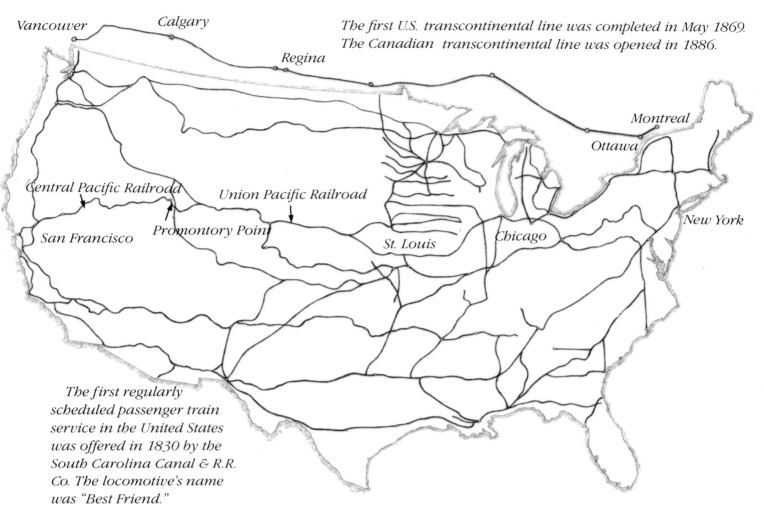

Vancouver   Calgary

The first U.S. transcontinental line was completed in May 1869.
The Canadian transcontinental line was opened in 1886.

Regina

Montreal

Ottawa

Central Pacific Railroad   Union Pacific Railroad

New York

San Francisco   Promontory Point

St. Louis   Chicago

The first regularly scheduled passenger train service in the United States was offered in 1830 by the South Carolina Canal & R.R. Co. The locomotive's name was "Best Friend."

It is easy for us to forget that before passenger railroads were invented, there was no way to get from one place to another except on foot, by horseback, or in horse-drawn carriages. Those who lived near rivers or the sea could travel by boat. You can imagine that in those days, people did not travel very much, nor very quickly or comfortably.

Suddenly, the steam railroad changed all that. People could travel easily and at low cost from one city to another. Raw materials could be brought to factories and manufactured goods distributed far and wide. The railroads helped business and industry and brought many people from the country into the cities to work in factories. In some countries, the railroads themselves quickly became the nation's largest employer, because so many people were put to work building new tracks and running the trains.

In America, the railroad provided a means of reaching the still undeveloped lands west of the Mississippi, and whole towns grew up around the railroad depots spaced along the line.

The locomotive did much more than save time for people, it expanded civilization.

Famous Locomotives

To determine which locomotive would pull trains on the new Liverpool & Manchester Railway, a competition was staged among several locomotives in 1829. This was called the "Rainhill Trials," and George and Robert Stephenson won with the "Rocket," at 30 mph.

The "Rocket" can be seen today at the Science Museum, London.

Great Northern Railway "No. 1" is on display at the National Railway Museum, York, England.

Describing the giant diameter of its single pair of driving wheels, this locomotive is known as an "Eight-foot Single."

The basic design of the locomotive hasn't changed much since it was first invented. Ever since then, designers have tried to make the original pattern better and better: more durable, cheaper, and above all, faster and stronger. Here are some of the most famous locomotives ever built.

An "Articulated" locomotive is one driven by more than one pair of two-cylinder engines separately mounted on the frame.

The Union Pacific "Big Boys" were the largest ever built, weighing 530 tons. Locomotives like this were designed for hauling long freight trains. A "Big Boy" can be seen today at Steamtown, Scranton, Pennsylvania.

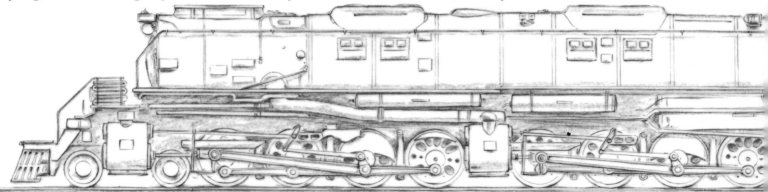

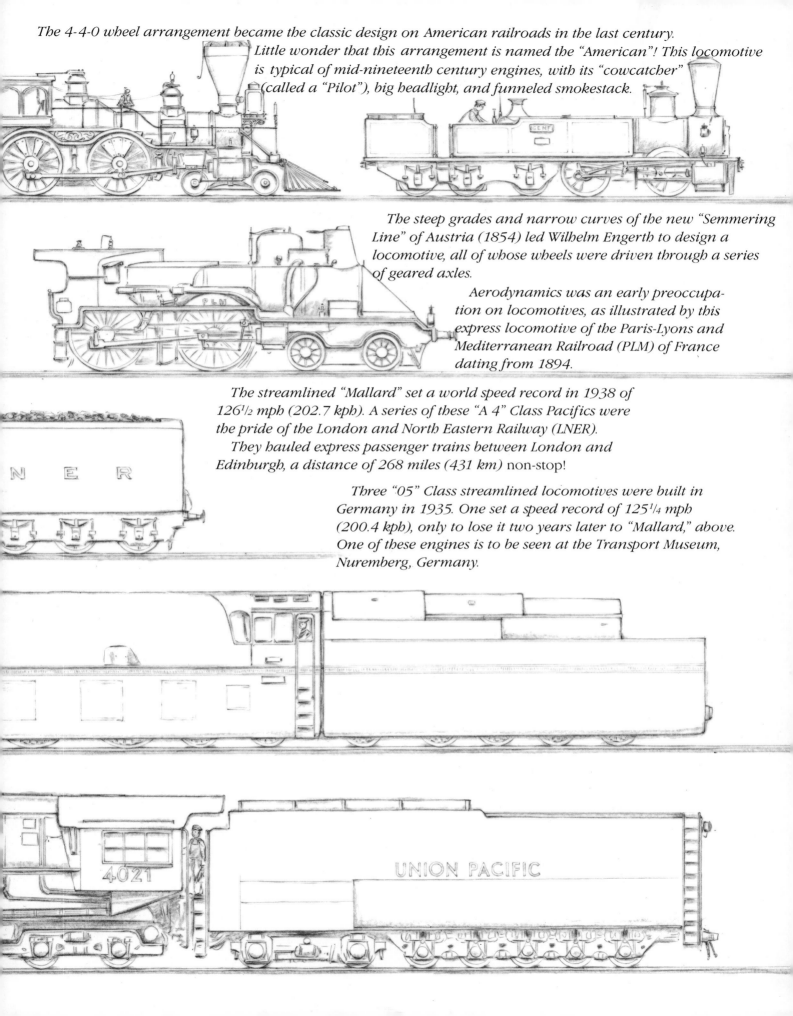

The 4-4-0 wheel arrangement became the classic design on American railroads in the last century. Little wonder that this arrangement is named the "American"! This locomotive is typical of mid-nineteenth century engines, with its "cowcatcher" (called a "Pilot"), big headlight, and funneled smokestack.

The steep grades and narrow curves of the new "Semmering Line" of Austria (1854) led Wilhelm Engerth to design a locomotive, all of whose wheels were driven through a series of geared axles.

Aerodynamics was an early preoccupation on locomotives, as illustrated by this express locomotive of the Paris-Lyons and Mediterranean Railroad (PLM) of France dating from 1894.

The streamlined "Mallard" set a world speed record in 1938 of 126$\frac{1}{2}$ mph (202.7 kph). A series of these "A 4" Class Pacifics were the pride of the London and North Eastern Railway (LNER). They hauled express passenger trains between London and Edinburgh, a distance of 268 miles (431 km) non-stop!

Three "05" Class streamlined locomotives were built in Germany in 1935. One set a speed record of 125$\frac{1}{4}$ mph (200.4 kph), only to lose it two years later to "Mallard," above. One of these engines is to be seen at the Transport Museum, Nuremberg, Germany.

The footplate on early locomotives was designed with little thought for the engine crew's comfort. What could be bliss on a summer evening was a test of endurance on a wet, wintry day!

Typical of many engines on the world's first railroads, the "Adler" was built in Robert Stephenson's locomotive works in Newcastle. A full-size running replica of the "Adler" is to be seen today in the Deutsche Museum, Munich.

ADLER

*The first locomotive in Germany, the "Adler,"
at full speed, in 1835.*

Steam Trains Present

A retrieved boiler and a set of wheels may be the basis for rebuilding a former locomotive. Here, boilers await attention at the Bluebell Railway, England.

Steam locomotives have all but disappeared from today's railroads. Sadly, as they were progressively replaced by electric or diesel-electric engines, most of the old steam engines were broken up for scrap metal. The few steam locomotives that were not junked have been saved by museums, where they receive much care and attention.

The Transport Museum, Nuremburg.

A number of famous locomotives are to be found in transportation museums around the world, many still fully operational.

Some locomotives have been rescued by groups of hobbyists, who restore them in their spare time and run them on short-line railroads.

There are still a handful of railroads around the world regularly operated with steam engines. They can be found in Eastern Europe, South America, India, and China. In fact, in China steam locomotives are still being built today.

In countries where coal is abundant, and labor inexpensive, steam still may be "king." In China, steam locomotives like this 2-10-2 "Forward" Class not only run daily, but are even being built at the Datong workshops at the rate of about one a week.

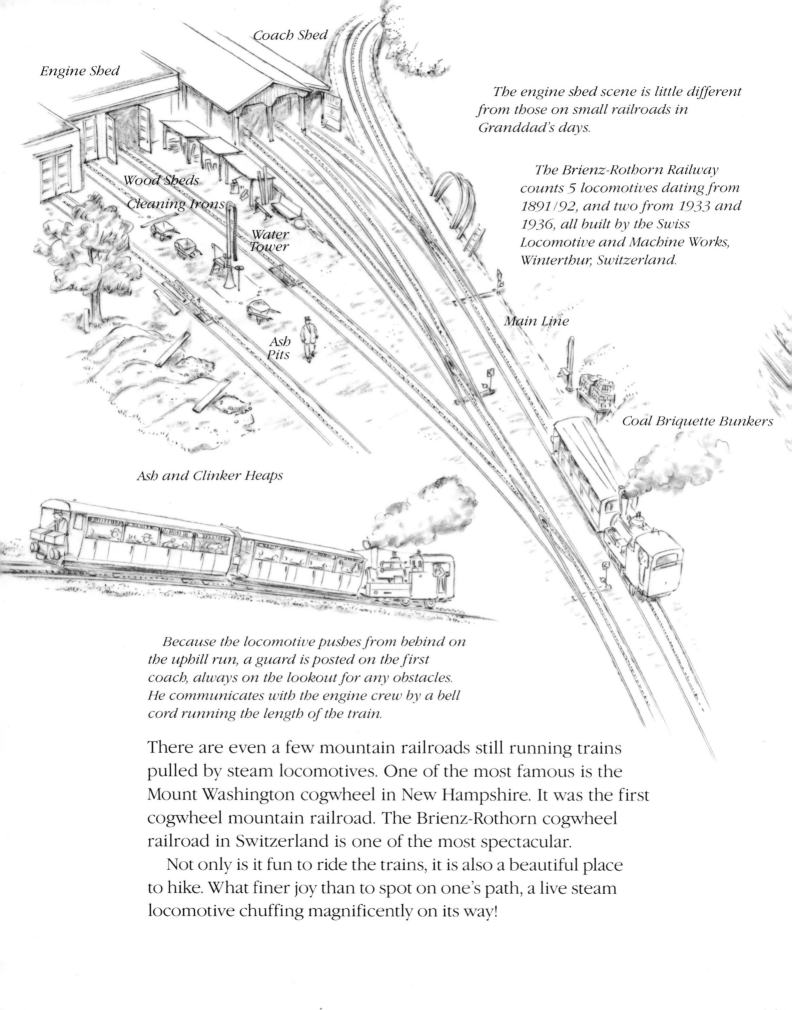

Coach Shed

Engine Shed

Wood Sheds

Cleaning Irons

Water Tower

Ash Pits

Ash and Clinker Heaps

The engine shed scene is little different from those on small railroads in Granddad's days.

The Brienz-Rothorn Railway counts 5 locomotives dating from 1891/92, and two from 1933 and 1936, all built by the Swiss Locomotive and Machine Works, Winterthur, Switzerland.

Main Line

Coal Briquette Bunkers

Because the locomotive pushes from behind on the uphill run, a guard is posted on the first coach, always on the lookout for any obstacles. He communicates with the engine crew by a bell cord running the length of the train.

There are even a few mountain railroads still running trains pulled by steam locomotives. One of the most famous is the Mount Washington cogwheel in New Hampshire. It was the first cogwheel mountain railroad. The Brienz-Rothorn cogwheel railroad in Switzerland is one of the most spectacular.

Not only is it fun to ride the trains, it is also a beautiful place to hike. What finer joy than to spot on one's path, a live steam locomotive chuffing magnificently on its way!

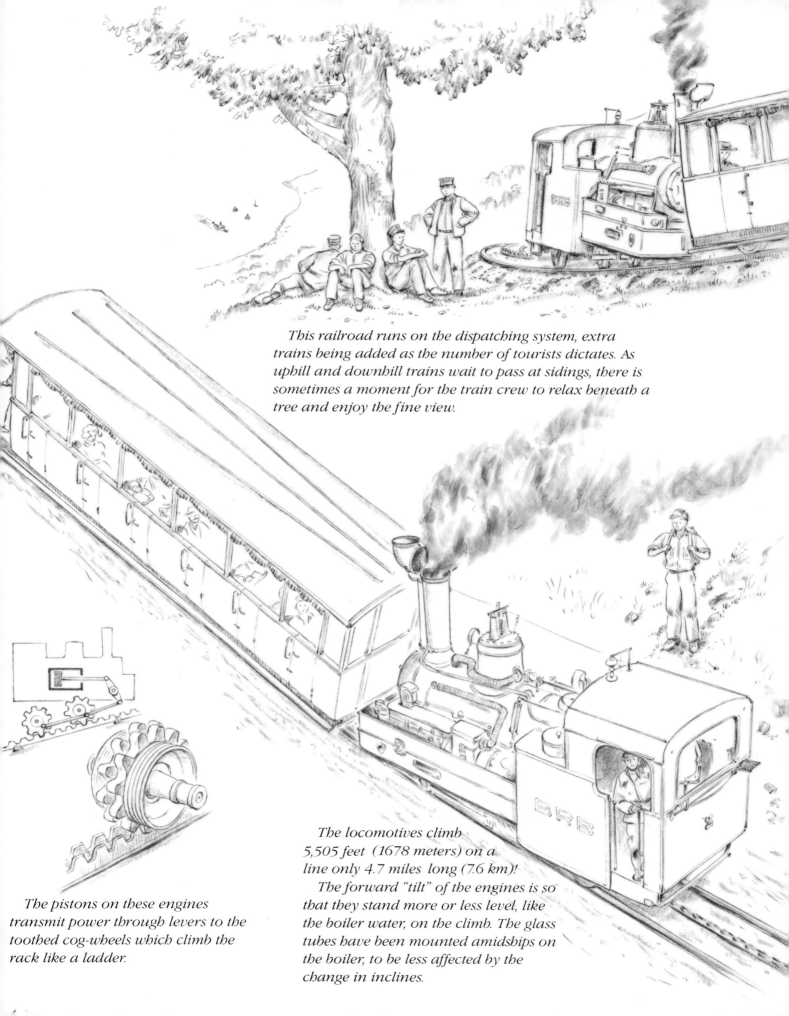

This railroad runs on the dispatching system, extra trains being added as the number of tourists dictates. As uphill and downhill trains wait to pass at sidings, there is sometimes a moment for the train crew to relax beneath a tree and enjoy the fine view.

The pistons on these engines transmit power through levers to the toothed cog-wheels which climb the rack like a ladder.

The locomotives climb 5,505 feet (1678 meters) on a line only 4.7 miles long (7.6 km)! The forward "tilt" of the engines is so that they stand more or less level, like the boiler water, on the climb. The glass tubes have been mounted amidships on the boiler, to be less affected by the change in inclines.

Atop the Rothorn.

Where else can one enjoy a view of snow-clad Alps, emerald green lakes, and a parade of white-plumed, chuffing steam trains!

Summit station, Brienz-Rothorn.
Altitude 7,360 ft (2244 meters).

Conclusion

A few rides on a steam locomotive made it clear to me why it is no longer a common sight on our railroads today. It is a costly machine to operate, because it burns a great deal of fuel and translates only a portion of spent energy into actual work. Even when it is not moving, a steam engine requires as much grooming as a racehorse, using up a lot of time and money.

Strictly speaking, the steam locomotive doesn't make much sense when compared to today's efficient electric engines, which are ready for service at the flip of a switch, and are powerful yet economical users of energy.

Yet, what impressed me most when I rode in the cab of the steam locomotive was the skill needed by the engineer and the fireman to keep a steam engine working. The slightest inattention to the fire, or a poorly set reversing lever might bring the machine to a standstill...while to ignore the water level could soon cause an explosion that would send both man and machine to a speedy end!

Those skills cannot be learned from a book, or even from a few hours in the cab. They require years of experience on the deck.

Sad as it is that steam locomotives have all but disappeared, it is fortunate that the number of excursion steam railroads is constantly growing, preserving the heritage of our industrial past.

It was heartening to see on all the locomotives I rode that there were always *three* people in the cab: the engineer, the fireman, and a young apprentice. It is nice to know that a child today can still rightly say, "When I grow up, I'll be a locomotive engineer!"

My thanks to:

Mr. Willy Biétry, Mr. François Bosshard, Mr. Sébastian Jarne, and the staff of the Blonay-Chamby Railroad, Switzerland;

Mr. Ernst Streule, Brienz-Rothorn-Bahn, Switzerland;

Mr. B. J. Holden, Mr. Ian Wright, and the staff of the Bluebell Railway, England;

Mr. Kelly Anderson, Mr. John Bowman, and Mr. David Griner, and the staff of the Strasburg Rail Road, Pennsylvania;

My Sources:

Although the number of books on trains is endless, there are relatively few readily available and easy to read on how locomotives are run.

The following were the most helpful to me:

How to Drive a Steam Locomotive, by Brian Hollingsworth, Astragal Books, London, 1979, and Penguin Books, 1981.

A History of the American Locomotive, by John H. White, Jr., Johns Hopkins Press, Baltimore, 1968, and Dover Publications, New York, 1979.

Fundamentals of the Steam Locomotive, Rail Heritage Publications, Omaha, Simmons-Boardman Publishers, 1949, 1983.

The Railway Workers: 1840-1870, by Frank McKenna, Faber & Faber, London and Boston, 1980.

George and Robert Stephenson, by L.T.C. Rolt, Longman, 1960, and Penguin Books, 1978.

The John Bull, by John H. White, Jr., Smithsonian Institution Press, Washington, D.C., 1981.

La Machine Locomotive, by Edouard Sauvage and André Chapelon, Librairie Ch. Beranger, 1947, and Editions du Layet, 1979.

Histoire de la Locomotion Terrestre: Les Chemins de Fer, by Charles Dollfus and Edgar de Geoffroy, L'Illustration, Paris, 1935.

Dampf am Brienzer Rothorn, by P. Cosandier, Brienz-Rothorn-Bahn, 1983.

Railroad Magazines
Railfan & Railroad, Carstens Publications, Inc., Newton, New Jersey
Trains: The Magazine of Railroading, Kalmbach Publishing Co., Milwaukee, Wisconsin

Railroad Museums
Railroad museums displaying steam locomotives are to be found in many countries around the world. It would be impossible to list all of them in this book, but here are some of the most famous:

The United States
California: California State Railroad Museum, Sacramento

Colorado: Colorado Railroad Museum, Golden

Illinois: Illinois Railway Museum, Union

Indiana: The Indiana Railway Museum, Inc., French Lick

Maryland: The Baltimore & Ohio Railroad Museum, Baltimore

Missouri: National Museum of Transport, St. Louis

Nebraska: Union Pacific Historical Museum, Omaha

Pennsylvania: Steamtown U.S.A., Scranton
          The Railroad Museum of Pennsylvania, Strasburg

Tennessee: The Tennessee Valley Railway Museum, Chattanooga

Texas: The Center for Transportation & Commerce, Galveston

Virginia: The Virginia Museum of Transportation, Roanoke

Washington, D.C.: National Museum of American History, Smithsonian Institution

Wisconsin: Rail America, Green Bay

For a complete listing of steam railroads and museums in the United States and Canada, see the *Steam Passenger Service Directory*, published annually by Empire State Railway Museum, Inc., Middletown, New York.

Canada
British Columbia: The Railway Museum in Cranbrook

Ontario: National Museum of Science & Technology, Ottawa

Quebec: Canadian Railway Museum, St. Constant

For other Canadian steam lines and museums, see the *Steam Passenger Service Directory* listed above.

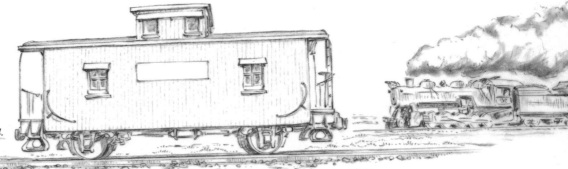

You can even rent a caboose for a night at Red Caboose Lodge, Strasburg, Pennsylvania.

Europe
Austria: The Austrian Technological and Railroad Museum, Vienna
Denmark: The Danish State Railways Museum, Odense
France: The National Railway Museum, Mulhouse
Germany: The Deutsche Museum, Munich
          The Transport Museum, Nuremberg
Great Britain: The National Railway Museum, York
          The Science Museum, London
Italy: The Leonardo da Vinci Museum of Science and Technology, Milan
Spain: The National Railroad Museum, Madrid
USSR: Railway Museum, Institute of Railway Engineers, Leningrad